Skysong

Skysong

DEL SMITH

Pentland Press, Inc.
England • USA • Scotland

*All carvings, photos, and sketches
are by the author.*

5122 Bur Oak Circle, Raleigh, North Carolina 27612
United States of America
919-782-0281

ISBN 1-57197-099-1
Library of Congress Catalog Card Number 97-75791

Copyright © 1998 Del Smith
All rights reserved, which includes the right to reproduce this book or portions thereof in any form whatsoever except as provided by the U.S. Copyright Law.

Printed in Hong Kong

Dedicated to Beatrice,

My wife for nearly 60 years,

Who is also

My very best friend.

Table of Contents

I Am the Red-Tailed Hawk 1
Wild Geese Calling 2
The Eye of the Peregrine 4
On the Wings of Eagles 6
I am the Great Horned Owl 8
I Am Raven 9
The California Condor 10
The Call of the Loon 13
The Great Blue Heron 14
I Am the Snowy Owl
    Bird of the Far North 16
The Steller's Jay 18
The Scarlet Macaw 20
I Am the Prairie Falcon 22
The Killdeer 24
The Red-backed Sandpiper (Dunlin) ... 26
The Bufflehead 27
The California Quail 28
Listen to a Different Drummer
    The Ruffed Grouse 30
Wilson's Snipe 33
The Last Passenger Pigeon 34
The Yellowlegs 36
The Roadrunner 38
I Am the American Eagle 40
The Brown Pelican 42
The Dance of the Cranes 44
The American Bittern 46
The Green Heron 48
The Water Ouzel 50
The Ruddy Turnstone 51
The Chinaman 52

The Scaled Quail 54
The Screech Owl 56
The Spotted Sandpiper 57
America's Skylark
    The Mocking Bird 58
The American Avocet 60
Dances on the Water
    The Western Grebe 62
The Trumpeter Swan 63
When the Curlew Cries 64
The Pygmy Owl 66
The Surfbird 67
The Snowy Egret 68
The Great Gray Owl 70
The Whooping Crane
    Symbol of a Lost Wilderness 71
The Magpie
    Bird of Complex Personality 72
The Virginia Rail 74
The Greenwing Teal 75
The Spotted Owl 76
The Black-bellied Plover 78
The Artful Dodger
    Cooper's Hawk 79
The Long-Billed Dowitcher 80
The Black Merlin 81
The Sparrow Hawk
    American Kestrel 82
The Black-crowned Night Heron 83
Funny Valentine 84
I Am Crow 86
A Gathering of Shorebirds 88
The Wandering Tattler 89

Foreword

Del Smith's carvings reflect his profound appreciation for the natural world and the force which it embodies. His work is a poetic echo of his concerns for the preservation of wildness and his understanding of the importance of maintaining the subtle balance necessary to support and preserve the richness he finds in the various habitats he visits.

His carvings capture a bird in motion, a frozen gesture or a bird at complete repose—in the midst of some wondrous preoccupation, dramatic action or intense focus—allowing us to glimpse a rare and beautiful aspect of bird life amplified by his careful attention to detail. Likewise, his poems are the result of careful observation, inspired by his wanderings through marshlands, the desert, fields, meadows and estuaries inhabited by his beloved wild fowl. His observations are reinforced by his careful combination of words and thoughts in an attempt to further describe his wonder, to capture his intuitive response and understand the true character of the individual birds he studies. Some are flashy, exuberant and dramatic, graceful, cunning, swift and daring, while others are small delicate, plain and ordinary—each personality and characteristic playing a crucial role in the overall balance of the life force.

His work spans a broad spectrum of symbolism and myth, most notably the associations, connections and mysteries described in the lore and mythology of indigenous native people. I am proud of my Choctaw blood; therefore I appreciate his sensitivity to and his understanding of this symbolism as yet another facet of his depth of knowledge of the natural forces which weave together conflicting symbols of pro-creation and fertility among omens of death—all balanced contradictions of the life force sometimes difficult to understand and decipher.

Through his visual and written descriptions of the Sandpiper, the Quail, the Heron, the Eagle, the Pelican, the Crow and the Raven he has allowed the viewer and the reader to enter his world of amazement and wonder, providing an invitation and an avenue to conspire with the forces of nature to better understand and appreciate those things he finds deeply meaningful and profound.

Larry Thomas

Dean of Academic Affairs
San Francisco Art Institute

Author's Note

It has not been my intent to describe these birds.
Nor to tell of their habits or their life-cycles.
But rather to capture something of their essence.

In doing so, I've shared the frustrations expressed by
noted Wisconsin Ecologist, Aldo Leopold, Author of
"A Sand County Almanac."

Putting these reflections into words
has required a great amount of thought,
of writing, of rewriting and of "cerebration."
A tiny yellowlegs writes a much better poem
each time it lifts a dainty foot.

Notes on Careers, Carvings, and the Photographs.

It all began with an old decoy, a gift from my wife as decoration for my den. I was hooked! I found the folk art aspects of antique hunting decoys, hand-carved in some old bayman's shanty rather than being designed and created in a factory, most appealing. Soon I was a confirmed collector. I had a hundred or more, some good, a few very good, but most of them mediocre. One day it occurred to me, "I think I could carve one of those." And I did.

Most of my working career was in the photographic business, first, as an apprentice in the darkroom, and later, as a photographer specializing, for the most part, in portraiture. It was years later in preparing a gallery talk for my first one-man show, that I came to realize just how much that early photographic training had influenced my carving. Composition, light and shadow, color balance and pose—all of these were certainly sub-consciously, if not directly, influenced by my training. Time out during World War II to work as a pattern maker and as a ship joiner certainly helped to hone my carving skills and manual dexterity.

This first one-man show also brought about my initial attempts to commit my feelings about birds to paper. Descriptive captions were essential. I wrote them. They were brief, but they certainly expressed sentiment! Doggerel? No doubt. However, comments about the captions compared favorably with comments about the carvings! Expanding on these captions came naturally and proved fascinating. I was soon deeply engrossed in the lore and the legends behind the birds I was carving.

In reviewing the notes I had written to myself in preparation for this gallery talk, I find reference to our Bill of Rights. Life, liberty and the pursuit of happiness in which I extoll the virtues of being driven. Driven to the point you miss carving when you've neglected it even for a few days; when you can't wait to get started on your next piece; when you go down to the shop to carve even if Monday night football is on the tube! Fortunately, I still feel "driven." I still feel "the happiness of pursuit!"

It was undoubtedly destined. Since my early childhood, I've been fascinated by birds—an interest more sentimental than scientific. At no time was I even tempted to consider a career in ornithology. I grew up around woodworking tools. My father worked his way through college, and later seminary, as a carpenter. Some of my fondest boyhood memories are of helping him build a flat-bottomed rowboat in our basement workshop one winter. And from eighth grade onward, I took all of the shop courses that were offered. (no homework!)

Long before the days of the "golden handshake," I opted for an early retirement, seeking time to pursue my many and varied outside interests. Perhaps above all else, I yearned for a return to rural Oregon from a more demanding life-style in Southern California. I knew it would be necessary to supplement our income. I dreamed of many possibilities. Bird carving was not one of them!

My first carvings were done during a period of sometimes stressful business responsibility, and undoubtedly reflected a search for therapy. Virtually all of my carvings were of waterfowl, and showed my keen interest in the old working decoys I was so engrossed in at the time. The first one I carved, a Canada Goose, was for the credenza in my office at Technicolor. It was being redecorated, and the choices of decor offered by the decorator were trite and unacceptable: An American flag attractively mounted on a small flagpole and a bust of Lincoln, if you were a Republican, or a bust of Jefferson if you were a Democrat!

I found an abandoned piece of an old telephone pole, patched the marks made by the lineman's spurs, and dispossessed a family of termites! I carved the head and neck out of white pine, detailed the entire piece, and gave it a natural finish. I still have it. My next carving was a present for one of my grandsons, and requests from other family members and friends soon followed.

These early carvings were "smoothies," sanded to eliminate any and all "imperfections." The first stages of the carving were done with a knife and a chisel. The marks left by the tools were very apparent. This somehow reflected a certain integrity which disappeared when the piece fell victim to the rasp and sandpaper in the smoothing process. My wife suggested that I paint one with the tool marks showing. I liked the results. Developing techniques to enhance this process came about quite naturally. For the same reason I enjoy seeing the brush strokes in an oil painting, I like to see the tool marks in a wood carving. Both clearly indicate the artist's hand.

I strive for sufficient realism, so that my carvings can readily be identified by species, but it's also my intent that they be recognized as carvings rather than as "wooden taxidermy." I do not create for the ornithologist, and have no strong fetish about absolute accuracy or infinite detail. I strive to capture the essence of the bird while observing Don Eckelberry's dictum: ". . . have the good taste not to smother feeling with technique."

Over the years my painting techniques and my carvings have changed. I assume this was due to a normal process of growth. Earlier works were mostly carved from sugar pine, a delightful wood to work with. But those who have used it know an undercoat is customarily used to prevent "bleeding." Even after switching from sugar pine and from "smoothies," I continued to use a sanding sealer or some type of undercoat and a final protective coating of thinned varnish was applied. The paint lay on the surface of the carving between these two layers. I have totally changed this approach to painting.

I'm not disciplined enough to use oil paints and cope with the long drying time required, so I settled on acrylics, used primarily in a watercolor technique of thin washes, with no undercoat. The wood (basswood) is kept slightly moist, allowing the paint to penetrate into the wood. A feather-like softness results. Final details are then added with a "dry brush" technique. No outer protective coat is applied. While perhaps susceptible to damage from excessive handling, the end results seem to justify this risk. (My carvings are not inexpensive. They need respect!) The care and feeding of a bird carving? Regular dusting with a featherduster—what else!

Quite a few years ago a magazine (I think it was *Sports Illustrated*) ran an article featuring a carving of a wild turkey. The bird was exploding out of a cornfield. It was magnificent, and extremely detailed! The cornstalks looked real, and each barbule showed on every feather. I have often regretted not living close to the museum where this carving is on exhibit, so that I might make a monthly visit to pay homage to the artists, a husband and wife team, who created it. But I would not want to live with it . . .

Usually, I try to carve my birds in a relaxed and restful mood. Someone once told me, "Del, your birds are all so loveable." I've never set out to carve a loveable bird! But I do try to carve each bird as if it were going in our own living room, as though I'd see it each day. I'd certainly want it to give me a good feeling—a relaxed, restful feeling. A friend has coined the phrase "animated repose," to aptly describe this attitude.

As the mount is an integral part of the finished piece, on major work it will often dictate what I will carve. In other words, on most major pieces I have to have the mount on hand before I can begin carving. Customarily, I will live with a mount for weeks, perhaps months, studying it to determine what bird would live there? What attitude would the bird express? I always strive to make the bird and the mount a single entity, and I'll often echo characteristics of the mount in the bird, or vice versa.

I'm constantly searching for suitable mounts. Contrary to common assumptions, I find very few on the beach, though we live close by. After they've been tumbled in the surf, the rough edges are rounded and much of the character is lost. Most of my mounts come from the bays and the backwaters where a ten-year high tide has left them stranded, left them to weather and to gather moss and to grow lichens. And it's surprising how many come from dry, high-desert country. The mounts are not varnished or otherwise treated. On some in our personal collection, we've kept a tiny ecosystem alive by occasionally watering it with a plant mister! Lichens have even sent up fruiting spores!

Early on I decided to utilize the years of experience I'd accumulated behind the camera and document the birds I created. The first photographs were taken with artificial lights in a studio. This soon proved unsatisfactory and gave way to a more natural setting. We feel very fortunate to live in an inspirational National Scenic Area on the Oregon coast immediately adjacent to a Nature Conservancy preserve. It isn't necessary to travel far to find attractive backgrounds. Matching the bird to its appropriate setting, however, is much more involved and has become a captivating challenge. It has meant trips far afield; to the high desert to photograph the Roadrunner and to the Columbia Gorge to set the Prairie Falcon amidst his favored rimrocks.

With my background in photography it is often assumed that I always carry a camera and photograph birds in the field. Not so. I don't even take a sketch pad along. My field work is to experience the birds, to observe them and to learn what I can of their lives, not really to study them.

Photographing birds would become a full-time undertaking and leave fewer hours for creative carving. It would also require infinite patience, which I lack. ("Controlled impatience" is my reply to suggestions that the carving and painting I do must require infinite patience!) There are many excellent photographers specializing in birds. I keep a file of their photographs and have accumulated an extensive library, much of it devoted to birds and Native American lore.

Also, over the years I have learned enough about bird anatomy to be aware of what's happening structurally when a bird lands or is flying a hundred feet in the air.

Especially when carving a bird for the first time, I try to have a mounted specimen or a study skin available, primarily for checking dimensions and the location of various feather tracts. Actual duplication of the mounted specimen could mean compounding errors—too fat, too thin, or whatever mistakes the taxidermist may have made.

I am frequently asked, "What is a study skin?" Serious students, customarily working under the auspices of some university, can get a permit to shoot a limited number of a given bird to conduct an approved study, for instance, of stomach contents. The university can perhaps use one specimen in the Natural History museum. The rest are then prepared as study skins for classroom instruction. Universities will frequently loan or give access to study skins to any serious carver. The study skins are very useful, but, nothing takes the place of field experience and simple observation.

I would certainly be remiss if I failed to express my deep appreciation to all those who have attended my shows, to my many patrons, and to the collectors—individual as well as corporate—whose interest and support has made the pain which inevitably accompanies creative efforts much easier to accept. An artist friend once told me, "If it doesn't give you any problems, in all probability it won't give you much satisfaction." I've had much satisfaction!

For those who are interested, all of the photographs were taken with a 35mm Pentax K1000 camera, most on 400 ASA Fujicolor or Kodacolor film. The lens equipment most commonly used was a Takumar 28-80mm zoom. Wonderful lenses and photo equipment are available today, some nearly automatic, and some that even give instructions! But equipment is not a substitute for experience. I often wonder, would anyone ask Hemingway what kind of typewriter he used?

Red Tailed Hawk—from the collection of Henrik Porter, M. D.

I Am the Red-Tailed Hawk

I have soared on the winds over these forests,
These rivers, and these sea-worn shores
Since before man arrived.

My earliest earth-brothers were gentle people
    of the Indian Nations.
They dwelt here before you came.
They, too, lived in all seasons;
With winter's cold, with ocean gales,
With summer's heat and the golden days of autumn.
They walked this earth with a very light tread,
And worshiped all of Nature.
But I've seen many changes . . .

This land is a land of great beauty,
And a land of great endurance.
I shall continue to enjoy it . . .
Forever.
Perhaps long after you have departed.

I am the Red-Tailed Hawk.

Wild Geese Calling

With the first hints of spring,
When the tree frog awakens and calls
    and the crocus blooms in the snow,
Earth-bound Man pauses;
He looks skyward and gazes into the morning mists.
Finally locating that wavering V,
He watches it approach, undulating.
Man feels the ancient urge of his nomadic heritage;
He is tantalized by that melodious, melancholy chorus
    echoing from the skies—
Wild Geese calling:
    "Follow me! Follow me!"
And he watches as they disappear into the distance.

Again in the fall,
When the hardwoods are ablaze with warpath colors
    and the air tastes of spice and of burning leaves—
Tangy, with a crisp, cold bite—
That clarion call awakens Man's ancestral traditions,
An inner restlessness inherited from an ancient past.
And once more Man feels the urge:
    "Follow me! Follow me!"

The Eye of the Peregrine

Man looks into the deep, dark orb of the Peregrine
       with fascination and with awe, spellbound.
The Peregrine looks back at Man, aloof and proud,
Totally unafraid, noble and haughty.
That alert eye has seen much of Man's quest for civilization,
For his name means "wanderer"
And in his travels he has known the ox-hide-covered fist
       of Mongol rulers,
Has grasped the carpeted wrist of countless Bedouin,
Has sat on the jewelled gauntlet of maharajas,
And has occupied the hand-tooled leather glove
       of medieval noblemen,
A symbol of their wealth and of their cultivated leisure.
Ancient Egypt saw him as the embodiment of Horus, God of the Day.
Upon death, he was embalmed, wrapped in linen bandage
       and prepared for eternity.
The curved throwing stick—
Fashioned from the graceful wing of the falcon—
Was a gift to the Hopi from Kisa, their Hawk God.

Man should also see, in that dispassionate eye,
The reflection of his own duplicity.
Sometime companion of the Peregrine, but often persecutor,
And despoiler of the environment.

Man, and DDT, brought a glaze to that once-bright eye,
Brought the Peregrine to the very brink of extinction.
But fortunately, that eye gleams again.
The haze is disappearing.
For the Peregrine is now protected;
Man is helping to restore him to his former glory.
Man can look into that eye, and he can feel good;
And the Peregrine will look back at Man,
Not with gratitude—for that is not the Peregrine's way—
But with poise.

Peregrine Falcon
–from the author's collection

On The Wings of Eagles

Sayeth the Lord unto Moses on Mount Sinai,
"Behold how I brought thee out of Egypt,
On the wings of Eagles."

Regal bird, bird of great power.
Proud emblem of Caesar's legions.
Emblazoned on his gilded standards,
And followed by tramping feet over much of the known world.
Bearer of the Emperor's soul to Olympus—
An idea borrowed from Ancient Greece.
Rome was eventually vanquished,
Swept into the dustbin of history.
But the Eagle flew on.

King of birds, bird of kings.
Hunting companion of Kublai Khan,
And Tartar hordes on the steppes of Asia—
A living arrow.
By the strict code of medieval Falconry,
Reserved exclusively for the Emperor's use.

Symbolic bird, bird of myth.
Ivan the Great (or Ivan, the Terrible!)
Gave the Eagle two heads:
". . .that you might look both
    to the East and to the West."

Aztec culture sought you out and found you,
Found you holding a serpent as prophecy foretold.
And they settled the Valley of Mexico.
In Yucatan, your effigy adorns Mayan ruins.
Exalted, you became Mexico's national emblem.

Bird of the Big Sky Country, land of long horizons.
From an eyrie high atop a lonely mesa,
Or floating aloft on summer thermals,
You survey your vast terrain,
Once home to the Plains Indian.
Out of deep respect and admiration,
He chose your feather to adorn his war bonnet—
A tally of his achievements and testament to his bravery.

Arrogant bird, haughty bird.
While civilization tries to brush you aside,
You remain,
Proud and stately . . .

And free.

I Am the Great Horned Owl

Bird of wisdom, Bird of doom.
Bird of Legend, Bird of gloom.
All nature shudders,
Grows silent at the sound of my voice.
And far back into the mists of time,
Man has huddled closer to his camp fire
    at the echo of my call in the night,
And he tells tales of my mystic powers,
For I am the Lord of Darkness.

I am the Great Horned Owl.

Great Horned Owl
–from the collection of
Dr. and Mrs. Austin
Connolly

I Am Raven

I have lived in many places.
I have known many worlds.
Most cultures thought me once-white.
Legendary are the many ways I became blackened.
"Oreb" to the Ancient Hebrews,
I fed Elijah in the wilderness.
Odin, All-God of the Norse,
Kept two of my kind as confidantes.
Viking hordes charged to do battle, and to loot,
Under the Banner of the Raven.

Through the desert to the oasis of Ammon,
Alexander the Great was guided by two ravens.
Yet when Noah sent me ashore at Mount Ararat,
I failed to return, and a dove took my place.

Northwest Indians hold me in awe.
Not divine, yet I am their Creator.
I discovered the People in a giant clamshell
And I set them free.
I stole daylight, fire, and fresh water—everything—
And gave it all to the People—sometimes unwillingly!
They think me a cunning trickster, greedy, and uncouth.
An amiable scoundrel;
But they are proud of Raven.
Look to their totems.

"Hraefn" in jolly olde England,
A member of the "Parlemente of Foules."
Legend says when the Ravens leave London Tower,
England will surely fall.
Winston Churchill clipped our wings.
We stayed. England stands.

I, too, shall survive.
Perhaps by trickery.

For I am Raven.

The California Condor

How does it feel . . .
      Being one of a handful,
      Unique, not because of achievement,
      Unique, as one of a mere handful left,
      Terminal survivors,
      Witnesses to a million years of evolution.
          How does it feel?

How does it feel . . .
      To come winging out of the Pleistocene,
      To have emerged in a land echoing with the deep rumblings
      of internal earthquakes,
      To cast your dark shadow over a land dotted with tar pits,
      With bubbling cauldrons of raw petroleum,
      Teeming with gasses vomited from deep fissures in the earth,
      Overhung by a perpetual cloud of steam,
      And peopled by ponderous creatures, not yet by Man.
          How does it feel?

How does it feel . . .
      To have watched this land slowly calm down,
      To see it inhabited by roving bands of Stone-Age hunters
      Frightened by the mighty forces at work in an awesome world,
      Struggling for existence,
      Yet outlasting many of your contemporaries,
      Watching as they fossilized.
          How does it feel?

How does it feel . . .
      To have watched primitive Man give way to the Indian
      Who made peace with his surroundings,
      And lived in harmony with the hills,
      Whose religion expressed respect for his environment,
      For all of the elements, and for all living creatures,
      Who watched you soar in his heavens effortlessly,
      And endowed you with supernatural powers.

Who painted your flying image on cave-wall and cliff,
And included your bones with his in burial—
That he, too, might be carried aloft.
But whose beliefs were dismissed by those of a lighter skin
As the "rituals of a heathen people."
    How does it feel?

How does it feel . . .
    To look down at Man and watch him become a lordly creature,
    No longer naked or clothed in skins,
    Convincing himself he's been granted dominion over all,
    Yet overlooking the responsibilities that accompany "dominion,"
    To watch him discover California, and your presence,
    And describe you with superlatives:
    "Huge and magnificently ugly!"
    Yet he wantonly shoots you and your kind.
        How does it feel?

How does it feel . . .
    To watch Man accelerate time,
    Flipping the pages ever faster,
    To see him cut your forests, dam your rivers, and foul your air,
    Ignore the obvious and spread chemical poisons,
    To watch lush grasslands—California of the Dons—
    Become citrus grove and oil field,
    Subdivision and shopping mall,
    Festooned with freeways.
        How does it feel?

How does it feel . . .
    To have forgotten your ancient instincts for survival,
    To have forsaken the drive to procreate,
    To assure the continuity of your species,
    To settle into a state of lethargy
    As the fire ebbs in your blood-red eye,
    To abandon hope . . .
        How does it feel?

And how will it feel . . .
> To be the very last individual,
> To fly alone
> Without mate or companion.
>> How will it feel?

When the final curtain falls, will it find you caged
Like, Martha, the last Passenger Pigeon?

Many of those who really care,
And are fighting valiantly to postpone the inevitable,
Hope it will find you free,
High in a big-cone spruce, itself a Glacial descendent,
In a remote and secluded corner of your once-huge domain.

Note:

Since this was written all wild California Condors (21) were live-trapped and three separate captive breeding programs established. To date successful reintroduction of seventeen birds has been accomplished in California and in Arizona. Because of the loss of habitat and with a total population—wild and captive—of fewer than 140 birds, the future of the California Condor is still very uncertain.

The Call of the Loon

Bird of the northern wilderness.
Bird of crystal clear mountain lakes.
Bird whose wild cry and eerie tremolo
    are the very essence of the north country . . .

Bird who in ages past, emerged from the distant time.
"Dodzina" to the northern natives.
They sing spring songs to the Loon,
Songs invariably answered.

Bird whose cry brings to all mankind a nervous tremor,
And awakens deep memories of an ancient past.
Bird whose haunting lament the Cree Indian believes
    is the cry of a fallen warrior
Denied entry into heaven.
Forever wandering . . .
Forever calling . . .
Forever pleading . . .

Common Loon
–from the collection of Margaret and John Griner

The Great Blue Heron

Majestic bird,
Bird of quiet dignity.
Bird sacred to the Seminole.
You grace our landscape,
Our tidal wetlands, and our coastal marshes.
Out of the mists your gray-blue form appears.
In complete harmony with your surroundings;
A part of them.

Silent sentinel,
Tall and gaunt and watchful.
Often on one leg,
Like a Maasai warrior . . .
Armed with a spear.

Patient bird,
Bird of graceful beauty.
Slow of movement,
And deliberate;
But lightening-quick with a rapier thrust!
Pity the unsuspecting fish who chances by,
For you are indeed,

Lord of the Shallows

The Great Blue Heron–from the collection of Mrs. Sydney Tremble

I Am the Snowy Owl
Bird of the Far North

"Ookpic" to my Eskimo neighbors.
A symbol of their good fortune;
For when I am present, the Silver Fox is near.

Down through the dim avenues of time
    Man has held me in deep respect—often fear.
I was the first bird depicted by Man
    on the smoke-tinted walls of an ancient cave,
With a stick and an amalgam of charcoal and blood.
Always my home has been in the barren grounds,
Land of pygmy willow and of stunted spruce,
Of the midnight sun and of permafrost.
I have advanced, and I have fallen back,
Governed by the slow, glacial ebb-and-flow of ice.
The Cree Nation tells tales of how I tricked Windigo—
Their Nemesis—and thus ended the threat of famine.
My feathers—"quiet as the murmur of the White Owl's wing"—
Bring sleep to their children.

But Man has not always been my friend;
Look to Man for the root of my shyness, of my silence.
For my sullen expression, and the glare in my lemon-hued eye.
But just as I have adapted to all changes
    since man emerged from that cave,
I shall survive.
In my own land of cold and of ice,
Of winter's perpetual darkness.
A land which few covet,
And where only the strong endure.
For I am a bird of the Far North.

I am the Snowy Owl.

Snowy Owl–from the collection of Art and Cheryl Lutz

The Steller's Jay

Listen for the raucous cry;
Watch as he half-flies, half-hops;
Branch to branch.
Upwards through the Sitka spruce,
Or flits among the alders.

In a shaft of sunlight,
Watch for the flash of a brilliant blue,
Dark, royal blue,
Bold against the varied greens of nature.
Look for the jaunty, black crest.
This is Steller's Jay.

Bird of many voices.
Sometimes a mimic, often a scold.
Bird of many moods.
Bold and gay;
Sometimes quiet and reflective,
But always furtive.
Bird of guilty conscience,
Even when innocent.

Noisy bird, vociferous,
Except at nesting time.
Then look for a silent, blue ghost
    drifting quietly through the forest,
Stealthy and secretive.

Bird of few friends.
Slandered bird.
Misunderstood bird.

The Steller's Jay–from the collection of Mr. and Mrs. Ken Folkstad

The Scarlet Macaw

Brilliant bird.
Bird of gaudy dress.
A flash of flame in lush, tropical forests.
Bird of Indian legend.
Bird of the sun.

The Pueblos traded turquoise for you,
Brought you from your home in southern jungles.
Pampered you.
More than an ornament—enshrined.
A God-idol.
Deified.
Worshiped.
For didn't the Sun Father use your crimson feathers
    to create daylight?
And aren't you charged with escorting the sun south
    to its winter home?
And north again for the Moon of Spring Planting?

Small wonder the Parrot clan in their kivas paid
    ritual homage!
And to a shaman, a fetish of your feathers
    became as a crucifix to a Jesuit Father . . .

The Scarlet Macaw—from the collection of Chuck and Pat Snawder

I Am the Prairie Falcon

For untold centuries I've climbed the western winds,
Soared aloft on thermal updrafts, then plunged earthward,
Hurling my wild cry of freedom at the rimrock below.

The once-proud Indian, who held title to no land,
Yet owned all of it, roamed my country.
Mountain men came, seeking the freedom I've always known.
I look down as a slow, ox-drawn wagon train winds
    across dry sagebrush flats.
An Iron Horse huffs and hurries along its shiny rails,
Trailed by a long plume of black smoke.
The Indian gives way to the rancher.
Cattle and fences replace the buffalo.
The first mushroom-shaped cloud appeared over my
    once-wild domain;
And I have felt the effect of DDT.
Yet I still live—free

For I am a Falcon.

The Killdeer

Listen to the cheery call
Of "charadrious vociferous"
Shrill and strident cry . . .
"Killdee! Killdee!"

Beautiful bird,
A delight to the eye.
Brown and ochre and lots of white.
Double neck-bands of black.
Disruptive coloration—
Camouflage at its best.
But throw in a bright red eye-ring
For class—
Or just for fun!

Rural bird,
Bird of the countryside.
Friend of the farmer,
And foe of his insect pests.
Least shore-bound of our shorebirds.
Fond of meadow, plowed field, and pasture.
Partial to fresh water in summer;
To the seashore in winter.
Mildly migratory, but home is almost anywhere.
And among the earliest sounds of spring?
Your welcome call . . .
"Killdee! Killdee!"

Nervous and restless bird;
Truly a plover.
Run a few steps,

Pause and call.
Look around you,
And change direction.
Run a few more steps.
Stop and snatch a bug,
Or pick up a weed seed.

Then fly off, skimming the ground,
And calling . . .
"Killdee! Killdee!"

Devoted parent,
Resourceful guardian of the home.
If immobility and camouflage fail,
Try bluster, bluff and vocal abuse.
But none do "distractive" display as well.
Few can better imitate a crippled bird.
Your broken wing is for real!
Draws attention from your precious nest,
Or your precocious chicks;
Who have frozen, or hidden under a leaf.

Killdeer's future is bright.
He's no longer hunted.
He's adaptable to Man and civilization.
His chicks often fly at thirty days . . .
Which leads to "double clutching."
He's not dependent upon disappearing wetlands,
And pesticide use is declining.
So perhaps we shall always hear that cheerful call . . .
"Killdee! Killdee!"

The Red-backed Sandpiper
(Dunlin)

Tiny sprite,
Bird of constant motion!
Bird of togetherness,
Seldom alone.

Gatherings of your kind scurrying in and out,
Flowing with the surge-and-retreat of the waves,
And looking like toy mice.
Have you no legs?
They're lost in a blur!

Taking wing for no apparent reason;
A wisp of alternating flashes,
Silver, then brown,
Banking and turning in unison,
Controlled by a single thought.

Circle and land again;
In and out . . .
Back and forth,
Hurry! Hurry!
Your energy fires need fuel!
The search for food never ends . . .

The Bufflehead

Tiny duck of deep waters,
Bird who loves the winter coast,
Who lingers longer . . .
Last to heed Nature's summons:
"North with the spring,"
Early to return each autumn.

Bird of fog-shrouded bays,
Of rain, and of mist, and of half-light.
Boldly clad in black and white . . .
Visible one minute,
Gone the next.
A deep-water diver.
Spirit duck of Indian lore.
Returned from the "otherworld"
Or denied entrance—
Who can say?
Bird of mystery.

Spirit Duck . . .

The California Quail

Listen to the cheery, three-note call.
It echoes across the valley,
And throughout the land of sagebrush and scrub oak.
The covey, keeping in touch,
Talking to one another . . .
"reach out and touch someone."

Sociable bird, happy bird.
Bird of togetherness and group living.
Enjoying the communal dust bath,
Or gleaning on the valley floor;
Huddled together on chilly desert nights.

Light-hearted bird,
Despite a lifetime under the shadow of the Cooper's Hawk.
Elusive bird; skillful at hiding.
At home on the ground,
But a strong flyer when necessary.

Adaptable to Man;
Almost tameable . . .
(If unmolested by the neighbor's cat!)
Proud parent who enjoys the family promenade,
In single file—Indian fashion.
Father in the lead,
With his jaunty, jet-black cockade tilted over one eye.
The tiny, Tom Thumb chicks next, at first invisible.
Then mother in her demure Quaker grays.
Always a pleasure to see;
Always a joy to hear.

California Quails–from the collection of T. and Grace Wilson

Listen to a Different Drummer
The Ruffed Grouse

Bird of the forest fringe—not the deep woods.
Bird of aspen, alder, and birch grove,
Of bracken fern and brushy thicket.
Bird of ancient ancestry;
Fossilized as far back as the Pleistocene.
Bird of subtle colors—
Of warm, earthy tones—autumn hues,
And of intricate feather pattern.
Bird of inherited habit.
Instinct says, "Don't run or fly—freeze" . . .
Cryptic coloration is reliable.

Bird for all seasons; nonmigratory, homebody,
Except during the "Mad Moon" of November
      when the family disbands,
The young leave home,
Driven by an ancient urge:
"Make it on your own,"
Which few do;
The strongest, the swift, the most intelligent . . .
And the luckiest.
For young Goshawks and Horned Owls are also on the move,
Equally determined to "make it on their own."
And winter brings the time of testing;
The "Moon of Hunger,"
When life is tenuous,
And habitat determines survival,
Even more than predation—
Seventy percent of the Grouse population perishes.

But with spring, life's cycle begins anew,
And the survivors are very prolific.
Sap flows upwards in the maple
    and buds burst forth.
The "Moon of Love" arrives.
Let the drumming season begin.

On his favorite log, the male Grouse struts.
He postures and beats his chest,
The very essence of wilderness splendor.
He tells the world, "This territory is mine!"
He hurls his challenge to all rivals,
And he offers passionate love to Lady Grouse.

The sound of drumming, elusive as an echo,
Reverberates through the woods like distant thunder.
It begins as a "hand-clap,"
Accelerates,
Becomes the rolling beat of muffled kettle-drums.
It lasts but a few seconds,
And is repeated after a brief rest.
For drumming takes tremendous energy.
Actually, a tiny sonic-boom—
Air rushing to fill a vacuum,
A sound below the hearing range of the Horned Owl—
Fortunately.
But Man can hear this seasonal summons,
If he will walk into the springtime woods,
Pause, and listen.

The Ruffed Grouse—from the collection of Tom and Lynn Dalton

Wilson's Snipe

At scout camp
You undoubtedly
Had an opportunity
To go Snipe hunting.

As a young tenderfoot
You perhaps felt it a privilege
To be included among the big guys . . .
Even allowed to hold the bag.

Though your Snipe never showed,
And you groped your way home in the dark—
Very much alone—
He's not entirely mythical.

Wilson's Snipe is the little fellow
Who was to have been
The "guest of honor."

The Last Passenger Pigeon

My name was Martha.
I died September first, 1914
At the Zoological Gardens in Cincinnati.
A curiosity, the last of billions.
"Beyond number or imagination."

We were once the most numerous bird on earth.
In vast legions, with neither beginning nor ending,
We roamed this entire country,
Feeding on then-abundant acorns and seeds.

"Wishkowhan, the Wanderer" to the Narragansetts.
They welcomed our coming each year,
And took only what they needed.
They left our nesting sites unmolested.
We prospered.

The White Man arrived, and our world changed.
"Manifest Destiny" drove us west—
Like the Indian.
The White Man developed a new market:
"Kentucky Fried Pigeon."

At a weekend trap-shoot in New York,
Twenty thousand of my kind were shot—
For "sport."
Sponsor of the event?
The Association for the Preservation of Fish and Game!

Market hunters came—a new "profession."
Honest men, working hard for a living.
They were resourceful, and very persistent.
They followed us . . .
Everywhere.
With swivel guns, sulphur pots, and nets.
Always the nets . . .
The telegraph kept them informed of our travels.
We couldn't escape;
No haven remained.
Dwindling forests cut our food supply,
But worse was the constant harassment.

Protective laws were suggested.
Lobbyists (even then!) were quick to respond.
They said we needed no protection.
"Extinction impossible."

Our huge flocks were decimated.
Broken up, scattered far and wide.
Accustomed to sheer numbers, we lost coherence,
Went into an abrupt decline,
Succumbed to the perpetual persecution.

But our passing left its mark.
Perhaps awakened—and shamed—by my death,
Conservation-minded people cried, "Enough!"
Game laws were quickly passed.
Too late for us.
Hopefully not for others.

Including Man.

The Yellowlegs

Listen for the cheery piping of the Yellowlegs.
It brings visions of brown and green beach grasses
    waving in the wind,
Calls to mind the pungent fragrance of salt marshes,
Of tidal mud-flats,
Visions of tiny lagoons, and of shallow streams,
Of small ponds and tide-pools.

Dainty bird, quick and nimble.
Surprisingly graceful on long, slender legs.
Delicate legs, thin legs . . .
Yellowlegs.

Unlike others of the Sandpiper Clan,
Rarely one to probe in the mud.
Rather a bird of the sandy shore and shallow water,
Darting here and there after killifish,
Bobbing and nodding in a jerky gait.
Sometimes hurried, always quick.
Swimming if necessary.

Driven north each spring by relentless urge
    from a home in far-away South America,
From Patagonia and the Pampas of Argentina.
Dressed, then, in warm browns,
Returning from the arctic in subdued shades of gray,
Having raised a family, feasted,
And stored energies for the lengthy return.

We watch your departure with regrets.
Give thanks for the migratory cycle.
It will bring you back next spring.

Yellowlegs—from the collection of Judy Kelly

The Roadrunner

Half-clown, half-idol.
Bird of myth and of sacred rite.
Bird of the "X" footprint . . .
Confuse your enemy,
Lead him astray.

Your feather on a moccasin toe
      makes the Zuni swift afoot,
Makes his path direct . . .
Like the flight of an arrow.

The cartoonist would have you a joker;
Outwit Wily Coyote. Beep! Beep!
But the People of the Pueblos know . . .
Roadrunner is strong;
Roadrunner has great endurance;
Roadrunner is the "Keeper of Courage."

Roadrunner–from the collection of Stan and Dee Little

I Am the American Eagle

Symbol of your freedom;
Figure of power and of majesty.
Token of your optimism and of your self-reliance.
Staunch emblem of a new nation with lofty aspirations.
I've graced your coin, your public buildings and your fighting ships
    as ancient relatives adorned the standards of Roman legions.

But I've had to retreat from your civilization . . .
Forced to seek a new wilderness
    where "home" can still be a wild and wind-swept crag,
And I can remain master of all I survey.

I am the thunderbird of Indian lore.
"White Cloud" whose feathers carry mystic powers;
Powers of war, and of healing, and of bringing rain,
Of granting courage and a successful hunt.
I was venerated, worshiped,
More than a mere symbol,
For I could vanish through a hole in the sky,
And go to the home of the Sun God . . .
I was the bearer of Man's soul to the heavens.
Though sometimes sacrificed, it was always with respect,
Never for "sport,"
And my forgiveness was sought.

Brother Salmon knew me as part of Nature's process of self-renewal;
For in Nature there is no mercy, no justice,
And very few creatures die of old age.
My only enemy has been Man.
But I shall continue as a symbol of your freedom.

For I am the American Eagle.

American Eagle–from the collection of John and Gwen May

The Brown Pelican

Absurd bird, laughable bird . . .
    but beguiling.
Outlandish bird, ridiculous bird . . .
    but endearingly charming.
Awkward ashore . . .
    a caricature come to life.
Aloft . . .
    a slow but graceful flyer;
    gregarious, a follow-the-leader flyer.

A stroke or two, a long glide;
A few more strokes, another glide;
Tilt your wings, fold them,
    turn and dive . . .
Disappear for a moment.

Enjoy your fish!

The Dance of the Cranes

A distant murmur in the skies;
Far-away music, tinkling bells.
Closer and closer, louder and louder.
"Those of the Gray Wind" approach
      amidst a crescendo of primitive trumpeting,
Like an ancient concerto hurled down from on high!
Sandhill Cranes have arrived at their dancing grounds!

Set pinions; dangling feet.
A dainty step or two upon touchdown.
Graze awhile; nod to a neighbor.
Circle and dance, slowly.
Comrades join, face each other,
And dance in a ring.

Ancient Man saw the Sun God,
Related your dance to fertility,
To happiness, and to longevity.

Circle and dance;
Toss a stick or a pebble aloft.
Dance faster, faster!
Sing a frenzied, passionate chorus!
Suddenly it stops.
All is silent . . .

Graze again.

Sandhill Cranes—from the collection of Northwest Natural Gas Co.

The American Bittern

We know Aristotle as a philosopher,
But he also wrote about natural history.
He has given us the legend of the Bittern.

A slave girl escaped and fled to the marsh.
She hid among the tall grasses but was found.
Her master ordered her whipped.
The girl died from this cruel punishment,
But her spirit returned to the swamp.
There she lives in solitude,
A recluse,
Determined never to be discovered again.
The stripes on her pale breast?
Lash marks from her fatal flogging.

The Bittern is still in hiding
    among the sedges and the rushes.
Occasionally, her deep call comes echoing
    across the silent marsh
    like thunder in the distance.
To this day she remains a frightened, secretive creature . . .

The American Bittern—from the collection of Major and Mrs. Ralph Morgan

The Green Heron

Silent bird,
Bird of quiet places;
Of streamside, creek and wooded shoreline.
Like the otter, a fisherman's companion . . .
Colorful bird, yet never flashy.
Bottle-green, russet, and creamy tan,
Black and yellow, and earthy browns.

Wary bird, yet unafraid.
Bird of seclusion by choice.
Adaptable to Man, if unmolested.
Bird of patience,
Bird of stealth,
Indeed a Heron . . .
Stalking,
Or waiting in ambush;
Armed with a spring-loaded dagger.
Hair-triggered,
And with unerring aim . . .

The Water Ouzel

The Little Dipper . . .
One of a kind.
Bird of somber attire, but gay spirit.
Slate-gray, with touches of umber.
Short, stiff wings, and stubby tail; Wren-like.
Up-and-down bobbing earns his nickname.

Bird of rushing mountain stream,
Of tumbling water;
Of spray-drenched rock or quiet pool.
Bird for all seasons . . .
Cheerful songster, in any weather;
Who sings in winter as if it were spring.
Bird who loves the icy water,
Garbed in special downy "underwear;"
Treated with high-viscosity winter oil,
Who walks into the stream,
Oblivious to frigid cold,
Literally flies underwater,
And walks on the river bottom,
Probing among the rocks and the gravel
    for caddis fly larvae.

Solitary bird except at nesting time,
Who then builds at streamside, often behind a waterfall!
Guards tiny white eggs
    in an oven-shaped bower of green moss,
Kept moist and kept alive . . .
Hatches precocious chicks,
Immediately at home in a watery world.

Ancient bird; here during the Distant Time.
"Nitsoo Taaneelot" to the Koyukon people.
Which appropriately translates:
    "Your grandmother sank."

The Ruddy Turnstone

Gorgeous bird, gaudy bird,
Bird of Peacock splendor.
Flashy bird, garish bird,
Tiny jewel of the seashore.
You with the coat of many colors;
"Checkerback" or "Calico-snipe."

Unlike your oft-drab, beach-bird cousins,
In disposition or attire.
No gentle probing with slender, delicate bill;
Rather flipping and prying at stones,
Seeking treasure underneath.

Proud bird, pugnacious bird;
Bird of tide-wrack and shingle shore.
Aloof, never timid,
Attuned to small gatherings, not flocks.
Your vivid hues and swagger-style
      lend color to our coastlines . . .

The Chinaman

Gaudy bird,
Proud and handsome,
Reserved and aloof.
Dignified of step . . .
With a touch of swagger.

Exotically Plumed;
With long, magnificent tail
    and chest of burnished copper,
Cheeks afire with crimson,
And collar of immaculate white.
The Ring-necked Pheasant.

An immigrant,
A stranger to these shores—
Like the White Man.
One of China's contributions to the West,
Along with the coolie;
Who wore a funny hat,
And a queue,
But built the Central Pacific,
And worked the mines—
For a pittance.

Ancient China saw a figure of authority.
Respected the pheasant—
As all authority was respected.
Dances for rain imitated the Pheasant;
Whose beating wings portrayed thunder.
China's "Thunderbird,"
Our "Ringneck."

Ring-Necked Pheasant—from the collection of Bruce Titus

The Scaled Quail

Bird of the desert floor.
Bird of mesquite thicket and dense cover.
Bird of the arroyo and of the Joshua tree.
Nature chose for your protection
    a delightful desert palette
Of grays and of umbers and of siennas . . .

Your neighbors, the Pueblo people,
Zuni, Hopi and the Navaho—
All loved your beauty;
Your sagebrush softness.
But they find you too secretive,
Too earth-bound to serve
    as a proper "Messenger to the Gods."

Perhaps it's just as well;
Along with veneration,
A sacrificial altar might have held your fate . . .

The Scaled Quail–from the author's collection

The Screech Owl

Bird of many voices . . .
Often a wail, seldom a screech!
Bird of the moonpath and midnight sky.
Bird of soft wing and of silent flight,
A cat with wings . . .

Bird of the totem and of Indian lore;
"I heard an owl call my name."
An arrow, fletched with your feather,
Flies silently to its mark.

Contradictory bird;
Omen of death . . .
Yet symbol of fertility.
Bearer of bad news . . .
With the soul of Man.
Misunderstood bird.

The Spotted Sandpiper

Listen for the loud, clear whistle
    of this graceful little wader.
Tiptoeing on a sandy shore,
Or balanced on a rock
    by sheltered waters . . .
Alone.

Nervous bird,
Constantly in motion,
Bobbing up and down;
"Teeter-tail" to many . . .
In flight—skimming the waves—
Nearly touching the water,
On wings that vibrate like a taut wire.

Solitary bird,
Unsocial bird,
Lonesome by choice.

America's Skylark
The Mocking Bird

Symbol of the South—
    of the deep South.
Romantic land of magnolia blossoms,
Of cotton plantations and Scarlet O'Hara
Of trees festooned with Spanish moss . . .
"Dixie."

A royal troubadour.
Mimic and minstrel,
Singing with gay abandon
    a joyous song;
One not always his own,
Sometimes borrowed
    from another bird, a cricket, or a frog—
Even a train whistle or screeching tires!
He shares his exuberance with the world,
Especially on moonlit nights,
When the neighborhood seeks slumber!
His repertoire and jubilant spirit
    help win Milady Mocker.

Sassy bird, fearless and feisty.
Bird who likes people—
But avoid the Mocker's nest!
Very territorial and protective,
Bold, daring, and tenacious.
High on family values.
And fidelity.
A wonderful parent.

A worthy example for man.

The Mocking Bird–from the collection of Mr. and Mrs. Jim Hetzler

The American Avocet

Bright and showy bird, conspicuous.
Awkward in appearance—a deception!
Bird of the open spaces,
At home on the broad, wet meadows,
The sun-baked mud flats,
The marshes, alkaline ponds, or the arid plains
    of vast western rangelands.
Disdainful of camouflage,
Of protective coloration . . .
No need to hide.

Changeable bird,
Quiet and indifferent,
Tame and unsuspicious.
Fearless bird,
Foolishly inquisitive,
But bold and aggressive.
A noisy brawler . . .
A true Westerner!

Gentle and concerned parent.
If loud and threatening cries,
Or bluff and bluster fail,
Try a plaintive call or fake a broken wing . . .

Protect those precocious chicks!

The American Avocet–from the collection of JoAnn Smith

Dances on the Water
The Western Grebe

The Swan Grebe . . .
Picture of aquatic splendor.
Most graceful of all diving birds.
Truly a water nymph,
Who swims with scarcely a ripple,
And dives with little effort,
Like sliding into the water.

Bird of elegant, silky plumage,
Of dark grey's and dazzling white,
With coal-black crest,
And eye of fiery crimson,
Armed with a javelin bill.
Aechmophorus, your Latin name,
Means "spear-bearing,"
But "Swan Grebe" better fits.

Bird of exotic wedding dance,
Of elaborate courtship antics,
Diving together,
Exchanging seaweed clumps
    while treading water breast-to-breast
Or madly racing across the water side by side.
Bizarre exercises . . .
"Pair-bonding."

Once decimated for the millinery trade . . .
At twenty cents per pelt—
Now protected.

"Thank you, Teddy Roosevelt . . ."

The Trumpeter Swan

Majestic bird, magnificent bird;
Bird of marshland, moist meadow, and mountain lake.
Graceful bird, pristine bird;
Bird of angelic whiteness.
Your trumpet call, resonant and mellow,
Like an ancient French horn,
Once echoed across our entire continent.

"Civilization" drove you west,
Hounded by Hudson Bay trappers,
Seeking swanskins for madam's powder puff.
You sought only seclusion,
Found it, finally, in the far north.
Winter calls you south,
But only as far as open water
     and finds you still wary of "civilization."

Faithful parent, proud parent,
Protective of your tiny puffs of thistledown.
Watchful as they grow,
Become "ugly ducklings,"
And emerge as royalty.

Driven to remote hideaways,
Man thought you lost,
Heard your "swan song" . . .
Prematurely.
He responded;
Gave you protection,
And wilderness set-asides.

Extinction, once certain, has been averted.

May your wild and haunting call, a symbol of solitude,
Always resound across America's wetlands . . .

When the Curlew Cries

To hear the Curlew's enchanting call
    is to watch gentle waves wash the shore,
To see beach grasses ripple before a soft wind,
To smell the pungency of the tide flats.

The ancient rhythm of migration remains a mystery.
What is that urge, that drive,
That pulse of eternity
    that tells the Curlew he mustn't tarry,
That he must hurry on to the Arctic tundra each spring?
Then calls him south, to sun-drenched, tropical beaches each fall
    after a too-brief pause—
Why can't he spend more time with us?

But he's always a welcome visitor;
Even though in autumn he'll leave us,
As Peter Matthiessen notes:
" . . . in solitude on an empty beach,
    with summer gone and a wind blowing."

Hudsonian Curlew—from the author's collection

The Pygmy Owl

Fearless bird!
Bird of diminutive size,
But tremendous heart!
Bird of benign appearance,
But bold and fierce!

Bird of half-light,
Of gloaming and the vesper hour
Of pre-dawn and the overcast day.
Seldom seen,
Except by the vigilant.
Ever-present none the less.

The Surfbird

Bird of crashing waves;
Bird of spray-drenched rocks;
Bird of the pounding surf
    and thundering seas.
"One who lives in the sea foam,"
Your Latin name translates.

Fitting you visit our Northwest Coast in winter,
Share in the violent storms.
But the seasons change . . .
The winds die down,
The waves subside.
The Arctic beckons
    with bewitching sweetness!
Brighten your colors—
Love awaits!—
And parenthood.

See you this fall!

The Snowy Egret

Bird of elegant beauty;
Most charming of the herons.
Dainty bird, exquisite;
Active and quick of movement.
Not a stalker or a patient waiter—
Most unheron-like.

Bird of pristine whiteness:
"Whiter than winter,"
Except for counter points.
An ebony bill, black legs, and yellow toes;
"The lady with the golden slippers!"
Courtship brings a "bridal veil" of lacy plumes
      to male and to female alike.
It brings a strong pair-bond.
Enhanced by constant display,
They are both very proud of their beauty,
And expressive of their love.

But "the Lord giveth, and the Lord taketh away."
As compensation for such visual elegance,
Comes vocal disaster!
A voice both coarse and guttural,
Raucous and loud.

Bird of togetherness, a colony nester.
At home in mangrove swamp, or coastal Savannah.
Bird with itchy wings . . .
A wanderer after family responsibilities fade,
But rarely one to travel alone.

Bird blessed with the curse of beauty—
Plumes the envy of all!
Indian chiefs met the conquistadors at Canaveral
      wearing Egret plumes of dazzling white.
Centers of the fashion trade,
London, Paris, and New York, eventually took note;
Aigrettes for a lady's chapeau . . .

Enter the plume hunter.
Millions of Egrets perished;
Entire colonies were destroyed,
Plundered for their plumes.
Little Snowy teetered on the brink of extinction.
An aroused public finally protested;
The Audubon Society emerged.
And the millinery establishment capitulated . . .
Reluctantly.

The future is no longer bleak,
Except as wetlands disappear.
Egrets are claiming their former homelands;
Some even moving to new territories.
Hopefully, their spotless purity
    will always adorn our landscape.

The Snowy Egret
–from the collection of
Stan and Dee Little

The Great Gray Owl

Bird of the deep, deep forest;
Phantom of the Far North,
From the land of black spruce and tamarack bog,
Of snow and of ice and of endless winter.
Largest of the owl family;
A deception—mostly feathers.
Feathers the color of lichens,
Of weather-bleached snags,
And of tree bark.
Soft feathers that muffle sound,
That bring silent flight;
To drift quietly through the trees,
Like a wisp of smoke . . .
Tiny yellow eyes set in large facial discs,
Give a quizzical expression,
Reflect curiosity—even towards Man.
Tame, unsuspicious, "perhaps even stupid" . . .

Evolved in the North Country,
And no longer strictly nocturnal.
Adjusted to the midnight sun,
And to perpetual twilight.

Nonmigratory.
Except periodically,
When the cone crop fails,
And the mice disappear,
And hunger drives him south—
But only to the fringes of civilization
    where man catches a glimpse of this apparition,
This Gray Ghost,
And yearns to know him better . . .

The Whooping Crane
Symbol of a Lost Wilderness

Bird of ageless wisdom.
Ancient bird, older than sapiens.
Relic of the near Pleistocene,
Who left fossilized footprints in the wetlands of history.
Whose remaining time is short,
Ultimately doomed and destined for oblivion,
In spite of Man's guilt-driven intervention.

Majestic bird, stately;
Long and deliberate of stride, like a gallant chief.
White as new-fallen snow,
But wearing a mask of black and vivid scarlet,
With piercing, lemon-hued eyes and uncanny vision.

Bird of marsh and of shallow water,
Unadaptable to Man's civilization.
Watchful and wary, shy and suspicious,
Conditioned by decades of persecution.
Once found nationwide,
But a stranger to recent generations.
Driven westward, ever westward,
Pressed by the tidal wave of Manifest Destiny . . .
His lands confiscated, like those of the Indian.

Bird of Aransas in winter,
Drawn to the far north each spring since the Age of Ice;
Heeding the summons of a mystic siren,
But pausing to dance along the way,
To celebrate the rites of spring,
And to fill midwestern prairie skies with a haunting bugle call.

Like our shrinking wilderness,
The Whooping Crane will be sorely missed . . .

The Magpie
Bird of Complex Personality

Bird of stark contrasts, of black and of white.
A jovial freebooter—
Born with street-smarts—a survivor.
Bird of few friends, disliked by his avian neighbors,
Detested by farmers, and despised by stockmen,
But admired by the Kiowas, the Cheyenne and the Comanche,
Who knew him well,
And revered by rain priests of the Zuni;
Essential to their precious gift of water.
His feathers, a talisman, a fetish,
Their badge of office.

Only bird who refused to enter the Ark,
Preferring to sit on the roof in the rain
     and jabber over the drowning world . . .
Therefore never properly baptized.

In faraway myth-time, a friend of Man;
Always willing to carry on a philosophical discussion,
To chat about the nature of things.

Constant tormentor of Coyote,
Abundant during the buffalo days.
Still fond of western ranchland,
Of the farmer's homestead more than open range.
Bird of the cottonwood grove, of back country roads.
Gregarious, but quarrelsome.
Suspicious and wary, but incurably inquisitive.
Quick to investigate any disturbance—
And participate!
Vain, gossipy, proud, and argumentative.
Despite years of persecution,
He enjoys the company of man!

The Magpie–from the author's collection

The Virginia Rail

Bird of the wetlands, bird of the marsh.
Bird of short wings and of tiny tail,
With long toes adapted to soft, moist earth.
Small wonder you run rather than fly;
Run and play hide-and-seek among the reeds,
Among the rushes and the cattails.
A living shadow in a land of shadows . . .
Phantom bird.

Bird of small size but subtle beauty,
Understated . . .
Bird of strange sounds;
A groan, a hiccup or a croak,
Sometimes even a shriek,
But never a song or a melody.
Bird seldom seen—
Except by those with patience!
But we know you're there;
We hear you!
Please come out,
Come out and be seen!

The Greenwing Teal

Dainty duck, handsome duck,
Named for an iridescent wing mark,
A "beauty spot."
Bird of quiet waters;
Dabbler in the shallows.

A tiny mite, diminutive,
Adept on land and graceful,
Yet swift of flight.
Gathering in flocks,
Flying in unison,
In close order,
Like your shorebird cousins.
Weaving and turning as one,
Undulating . . .
Wisps of smoke.

Or just "dropping in."
Alone and unannounced . . .

The Spotted Owl

Always uncommon, now endangered.
Bird whose home is the old growth forest,
But whose fate is being determined in the courtroom,
And debated in the halls of congress.

A focal point of frustration,
Defended by the environmentalist;
By the Wilderness Society and the Sierra Club.
Innocent pawn in a power struggle;
Disliked by some,
Loved by many.
Known by few.

Bird of solitude, bird of the dense forest.
Shy and quiet bird, seldom seen.
Silent as a shadow in a world of shadows.
Sleepy and can't-be-bothered by day,
Alert and active at night.

Plumage of rich and vibrant browns,
In a delicate tapestry.
Soft as velvet,
And spotted, of course . . .

Inquisitive, dark brown eyes
    and an endearing expression
    belie his occupation—predator.
Ask the chipmunk or the flying squirrel.

Bird with a message for Man,
Like the Coal Mine Canary.
Indicator bird,
Barometer of the forest community's health.
By his threatened extinction, he warns Man to pause,
Move cautiously—
Don't destroy your world.

Mild-mannered bird.
Bird of gentle movement
    and quiet disposition.
Curious, unsuspicious and tame . . .

Seeking only solitude and refuge,
Yet garnering fame and notoriety . . .
And headlines.

The Black-bellied Plover

Dignified and imposing;
Aristocrat among birds of the shore.
Strikingly beautiful in springtime garb,
Ebony and white, in bold pattern.
Wary and hard to approach . . .

A creature of the tides,
Like all of your Plover cousins.
High water finds you at rest, with companions,
Among marsh grasses at water's edge.
When low tide exposes the pungent mud flats,
Leaving replenished nutrition from the sea,
You're first at the feast!

Run a short distance,
Stop . . .
Look around you and probe.
Change directions;
Run a few more steps,
Robin-like . . .
Then cry a wild, plaintive, musical whistle,
Sweetest of all the Plovers,
And fly away . . .

The Artful Dodger
Cooper's Hawk

In Man's not-too-distant past,
When unfenced farm flocks were the rule
      rather than the exception,
Cooper's Hawk found barnyard fowl easy prey,
And "finger-lickin' good!"
Having acquired these gourmet tastes,
He became the "original formula" Chicken Hawk—
Generic . . .
A bold and brash farm yard raider;
Daring and crafty and furtive.

Man, of course, reacted;
Cooper's Hawk triggered his distrust,
His animosity towards the Hawk family in general.
These memories fade slowly,
But a truce has been called.
Cooper's Hawk is now protected,
By law, if not always by practice.
But his years on the lam had their effect;
To this day, he's stealthy, elusive, and very secretive.
A bird of subtle beauty,
Seldom seen . . .

The Long-Billed Dowitcher

"Upon ye beach
They spied great multitudes
Of birdes of manie kindes,
They being there
To pick up ye fat wormes
And little fishes.
They have long bills wch they thrust
Into ye little holes in ye sand
And pull up ye fat wormes
With great relish.
Ye beach birdes are verrie shy
And quick a-wing . . . ."

Obadiah Turner's journal
Lynn, Massachusetts – 1638

The Black Merlin

Bold bird, bird of dash.
Fearless bird, swift flyer.
In love with open country,
With moorland and marsh and seashore,
Sand dune and coastal grasslands.

"Milady's Falcon" in days of yore;
Often in court, on a bejeweled glove.
Among your legion of admirers,
Number Catherine, the Great;
And Mary, Queen of Scots.

To the Merlin, much of the world is home;
But you of the dark phase—melanistic—
Abide only along Pacific Northwest shores.
We bid of you,
"Please stay with us—always!"

The Sparrow Hawk
American Kestrel

Frolicsome Falcon,
Lighthearted bird.
Beautiful and of jaunty spirit,
Enjoying an unfettered freedom on carefree wings . . .
Life gives you so much pleasure!

Devoted parent;
Brave, not fierce.
Time-honored tradition among falconers
      respects your gentle disposition.
Ideal for the young nobleman—
His very first Falcon . . .

Man envies your flying skills;
Your lilting flight,
Your ability to hover in mid-air, wings a-flutter,
As if suspended on an unseen string.
You revel in the sheer pleasure of flight,
And make flying seem such a joy . . .
And oh, so simple!

The Black-crowned Night Heron

Bird of dusk,
Bird of twilight,
And of the full moon.
Bird of early morning mists,
And of the overcast day.

Why does he do his fishing at night?
Who can say?
Perhaps his ancestors—
In common with most fisherfolk—
"Just had to get in one more cast!"

Funny Valentine

The generic Owl.
Haunter of vacant houses,
Of old barns, and belfreys, and church steeples.
Bird of stygian darkness,
Infernal, gloomy, sinister,
And very nocturnal!
The Barn Owl.

Pale colors and silent flight
    against a moonless sky,
Bring to mind a fluttering shroud,
Invite superstition,
And misunderstanding.
Messenger of death and evil omen,
Or symbol of wisdom and good luck.
Primitive cultures have chosen both,
So take your pick.

Build a better mousetrap?
No way!
A Barn Owl with a hungry brood
    is worth a dozen cats!
It's a fortunate farmer
    whose barn hosts the Funny Valentine;
She'll pay her rent . . .

The Barn Owl–from the collection of Dee and Ann Roby

I Am Crow

But you know me not;
Only "as the Crow flies",
Who lives in "the Crow's nest," and "Crow-hops."
"To eat Crow?" Unthinkable!

You believe me an incorrigible scalawag,
Brazen, insolent, and irreverent,
Yet you admire my intelligence,
But you know me not.

I am Crow.
Completely black,
Three dimensional black—
Black, the color of mystery.

I am Crow.
A medicine bird;
Little sister of Great Raven and Earth Mother.
I am their emissary to and from the spirit world.
They have given me powers to quiet the unquiet dead.

I am Crow.
Sacred bird of the Ghost Dance.
Trusted to carry the prophet's message;
A prayer for peace and restoration,
Which was misunderstood.
Thought to be a dance of war,
The Ghost Dance was prohibited.

I am Crow.
Honored by the Cheyenne and the Arapaho,
And respected by all who knew me well.
I brought seed corn to the Algonquins,
A gift from the Great Creator.
They don't begrudge the little I steal back;
They see no need for "scare crows."

I am Crow.
I foretold the coming of the White Man.
Perhaps I shall be here after he is gone;
For I am crafty.
I am a survivor.
I am Crow.

A Gathering of Shorebirds

Happy sounds!
Joyous sounds!
Cheerful sounds!

A band of small shorebirds
    chattering with one another,
Scurrying about on the hard, wet sands
    like tiny, wind-up toys,
Or calling back and forth as they fly past;
Alternating flashes of gray and brown and silver
    as they bank and turn in unison.
Sharing a common pulse;
Sharing the same heartbeat . . .

The Wandering Tattler

Lonely bird, lonely by choice;
Satisfied with its own company.
Nervous bird, restless bird,
Constantly on the move.
At home on spray-drenched, offshore rocks,
Or coral-encased South Sea lagoons.
In love with rocky northwest headlands,
And the fog-enshrouded coast
    which suits your mousey-gray wardrobe,
Yet you yearn for sunbathed, tropic shores,
And seek them out . . . far away.

Your loud ringing whistle,
That shrill, quavering alarm-cry,
Has earned your family name, "Tattler."
Your nomadic travels make you the "Wanderer"

What romantic places you visit each year!
The Bering Straits and Siberia.
The Aleutians.
Mindanao, Kauai, Acapulco and Fiji.
The Society Islands and all of Oceana.

Man covets your footloose freedom!